IS THIS ADULTING?

Growing Up Millennial and Uncovering our Authenticity

MARGI SCOTT

Is This Adulting?
Growing up Millennial and Uncovering our Authenticity
©2023, Margi Scott

ISBN: 978-1-66789-995-4
ISBN eBook: 978-1-66789-996-1

TABLE OF CONTENTS

FOREWORD

It's Loud in Here — A message to my fellow Millennials

After 7 years of writing, deleting, re-writing, deleting, and writing some more, I am submitting this manuscript the night after yet another school shooting in the US. I am depleted, angry and mourning for this country. Part of me wants to delete and rewrite again to stay relevant to what we all need in this moment. The truth is our collective pain and disconnect is something we all feel in one form or another. We need each other. We know how to connect intimately with each other from a place of authenticity deep within our marrow, yet we are so overwhelmed by the NOISE around us that we often subconsciously choose the next distraction offered to us and move on because the pain is too much to process. That is understandable.

I want this book to be a message of hope. A love letter to my generation. A call to action because we do not need an invitation to do things differently. To change our minds or our programming. To hone into the feeling of freedom and empowerment that we might have known as kids and bring it to today's experience. We are designed to create, connect, grow, and build. Our world and our children need us to dig deep and find the parts of ourselves that have been coated in trauma from the past three years or beyond and numbed to the adaptation of finding social validation through dance videos and rants for our "target audiences." We need to break out of this mold and we can absolutely do it, together.

I hope this book brings you humor and strength. In its short text I pray you find some inspiration and possibly some new perspective. This exploration goes beyond us uncovering our authenticity. We must break out of the lanes we are expected to be in to continue to create the positive change that our generation will be known for. We are the adults in the room, and we cannot rest in defeat. Let this book remind us to care for each other, to care for ourselves, and to look inward for the calling and truth that God has put on our hearts. I promise this whole book will not feel this heavy, but I pray it lands in a grounded authentic way for you.

As you read, if you are called to get quiet, put on a song, write in your journal, or go for a walk in the woods, do it. At least once during this book, allow yourself some time to internalize and process in the quiet. We are a generation of humans who grew up with boredom. Playing in our rooms, talking to ourselves in the mirror, spinning on the recliner listening to a busy signal, trapsing through the woods pretending we were on survival missions, or swimming in the pool for hours pretending we were dolphins with the occasional pause to discuss the meaning of life. Allow your brain the space to listen and indulge in the push to create or express through art, physical expression (running, dance, punching inanimate objects), touch, voice, music, wonder, meditation, prayer or tears. Let it out. We are a generation who needs release. Let's decide right here to support each other in that way.

We are bigger and more powerful than the options society presents to us. Our authenticity is a blessing we bring to this earth. We need to start by understanding what it means to be authentic, real, in our truth. Then we can bring it forward and in doing so we connect with something greater than ourselves. In our textual understanding of God, he has always done his work in partnership with human beings. This power is available to us as we show up in humility and in authentic acknowledgement and honoring of who we are. No changes needed.

Thanks for picking up this book. Read it, share it, let's talk about it. Millennials are changing the world for the better every day just by showing up as themselves. You are doing that too. Let these words cheer you on in your journey. Onward!

INTRODUCTION

Trigger Warnings:

God- You will find this name in this book. If you picked up this book, you're probably an adult or on your way to becoming one. I am going to go ahead and spare you the definition of God often presented to make everyone in the room comfortable. I will also skip giving you some sort of awkward permission to call him whatever you want as you have most likely have already read that same disclaimer in every self-help book you've picked up ("I call Him God, but you can call him the Universe, etc…). I have a relationship with God and recently I've been challenging myself to bring more of that crucial side of me to everything I do.

Through my exploration of authenticity in life and while writing this book, I came face to face with God's truth many times. It is impossible for me to connect to my authenticity without hearing from or being nudged by God in some way. I originally wrote a whole chapter on "Spirit" and I was so grossed out by my own placating nonsense that after re-writing it three times I deleted it completely.

I do not use my faith to categorize myself, but my faith is part of who I am and why I am here, and I can't talk about authenticity without bringing God into it. I tried that too- it sucked. It is not truthful for me to leave God out of my story. I also refer to God as a "He." This is not because I believe God is a human with male genitalia sitting in the sky watching us. It is because although the original word for God in the Hebrew bible, Yahweh, did not assign masculine or feminine gender; Elohim, which was later also used to name God, is masculine. Biblical text was later translated to Greek then English and took on a on a masculine pronoun (think LE café verses LA musique) and is referred to as Father, etc. To be clear, God in his being is BOTH feminine and masculine.

You have the freedom to believe whatever you want and those beliefs are truly welcome here. Just because you are reading this book does not mean I expect you to agree with all of it.

I fully admit that Christians have collectively made a rough name for ourselves in this country. Perhaps you have been hurt or judged by the church, by organized religion or by a religious person in your own journey. I certainly have. My [personal] *faith* does not misuse Jesus's teaching and God's word to abuse humans and ostracize "others." We are each other. We are the same. To me, faith is a personal journey and organization around it should benefit as a space for community, inclusion, truth, education, and positive change.

The hurtful behavior that very much exists, however, is a result of humanity and our desperation to categorize ourselves and avoid our own shame by pointing out what we believe is wrong with others. It is a small way of thinking which has a huge effect. It destroys relationships and demoralizes those we are called to love.

That destructive nonsense is not a reflection of who God is. As the ghost of Christmas Present says in Charles Dickens' A Christmas Carol when speaking as a representative for God,

"There are some upon this earth of yours who claim to know me and my brothers, and do their deeds of ill will and selfishness in our name. These so-called "men of the cloth" are as strange to me and my kin as if they never lived. Charge their doings to them, not us."

Enough on that for now, God certainly does not need me as a publicist.

Swearing- I cuss like a sailor, and it's an ugly habit, but it's a cheap way that I express myself. I have challenged myself to use foul language only when necessary and to indicate it only with the first letter of the word (my editor later advised against this). Occasionally, the whole word makes the page. I hope you're still reading at this point.

Generalizations- I make some sweeping generalizations about millennials, older millennials, women in the workplace, men in the workplace, humans on social media, folks who pretend to have unique thoughts, etc. I know "not everyone is like that," but if you find yourself feeling defensive about one or more generalizations, you may fit the description. Allow yourself to keep an open mind and enjoy this book. It's ok to find humor in our collective ridiculousness.

Anecdotes- If you came here for all the answers, you may be disappointed. I wrote this book because we need a different conversation in many corners of our older millennial lives. In this moment where everyone is talking, and nobody is really saying anything let alone listening, we need a clearer path to finding our authentic selves to bring our unbridled magic to the world. Maybe I will end up writing a longer, more focused book(s) on one (or many) of these topics, but we need to start somewhere. This book is about restarting a bunch of the crappy narratives in our society but not necessarily finishing those conversations. I don't have all the answers to some of the bullshit in our culture, but I do see a need to uncover it.

Politics- I don't really discuss politics, but there is a moment in this book where you may think I am taking that turn. Keep going- it's an important part and it is incredibly brief. I promise.

Also, for the record, I am not a doctor, nor do I pretend to be. I am slightly, potentially obsessed with all things health-related, and I talk about my journey through *some* of those pathways throughout this book, but I am not making official recommendations for anyone because I don't have the credentials to do so. We are all different, and we all need different things to address our very different bodies, minds, and souls as we stride toward optimal health and continue to grow. Do your own research, and please [dear God] do not trust me to diagnose you with anything. Ever.

There are suggestions, calls to action, and exercises in this book and I kept it right at 30,000 words because we all know us older millennials have shit attention spans and need to be constantly entertained (the version you are reading was cut down to a 20,000 novella/eBook - even the most distracted millennial should be able to make it through). So, grab a journal and a pen, pause your current Netflix binge, and let's get into it!

WHAT THE AF IS AUTHENTICITY?

My Twelve-Year-Old Self

I walked into the house still in my bathing suit with bags of presents hanging from my arms and ran straight upstairs to my room. I dropped my gifts on the floor and plopped onto my bed, exhausted from a day of sharks and minnows, snacks, cake, and belly laughs with my friends. It was the best birthday to date. I moved down to my floor and sat on my fuchsia carpet, surrounded by new treasures. Among the impressive pile included an assortment of lip smackers, cash, a purple and teal Tamagotchi pet, and the gift I remember the most vividly—a gift basket including shower gel, a yellow loofa, and a full-sized bottle of "Sunflower" by Elizabeth Arden Eau de toilette. I made it.

After what felt like centuries of body spritzes and attempting to stick out in a crowd of "Sun-Ripened Raspberry" body lotion, I had finally scored my first real "perfume." With this gift set, I would be able to follow the instructions I had received in my first copy of *Seventeen* only a month prior. I would LAYER the fragrance—Shower gel, then spritz the eau de toilette for lasting effect and be known as "that girl" who smelled irresistible at the next 7th grade dance, or as we called them, "Boy Scout Dances."

These dances were held by the boy scouts, who at the time could be identified by their long mushroom-cut hairdos, Smashing Pumpkins t-shirts, and baggy wide-legged jeans. As middle schoolers, we lived for those Friday night grind lines to "No Diggity" in the elementary school cafeteria amidst the waft of bleach, garbage, and hot, preservative-filled food. The girls would gauge the night a success based on how many slow dances we took part in, to songs like "All My Life" by K-Ci & JoJo or "I'll Make Love to You" by Boyz II Men.

The Boy Scouts would always make sure the night ended with an eight-minute rendition of "Stairway to Heaven," during which they would sway around a bit near the speakers in a prayer-like ritual. The rest of us made sure to send our friends off as messenger pigeons to members of the opposite sex to confirm who liked whom, or when we would be settled at our sleepover locations to promptly log on to AOL and finish what was started during the slow dance to "Butterfly" by Mariah Carey.

This gift set of "Sunflower" was sure to make Jason regret the time he asked me to be his girlfriend during a round of truth or dare on the ski bus and then pretended like we had never met when he returned from vacation a week later. I had grown up. I took the basket into my bathroom, which was filled to the brim with every bath and body product I could snag with my allowance during the spare time I spent weekly perusing the aisles of Woolworth's before dance class. I looked into the mirror and smirked at my bad self. With Sun-In bleached frizzy/ curly hair, multicolored braces, and bloodshot hard contact-wearing eyes, I spritzed the yellow liquid onto my wrist. I immediately felt like the supermodel I was. I had invented glamor at that moment. Much to my chagrin, Shawn did not propose at my locker that September. Everyone was still "going out" with someone, except me.

"Sunflower" joined fragrances like "Curve" and "Ralph" as the signature fragrances of the 90's. It turns out I didn't invent that surreal vibe I experienced in my fruit-wallpapered off-mauve bathroom when I whiffed my new fragrance for the first time. That exact moment was invented for me in a marketing office at Revlon. I was a follower, a copier, a target market, but, to me, that moment was authentic. By engaging with a material possession that created an emotion in me, I connected with a side of my personality that I had previously only expressed through my building my established rock collection or earing money from budding friendship bracelet business (thank you to all of my family members who placed orders during the OBX family reunion of 1995).

The product in my hand was not creating my authenticity, but my relationship to self-worth and expanded confidence was continuing to develop as a pillar of my personality. I had elevated my experience in one moment. It was affirming a side of me that already existed. A side of me that was emerging and ready to grow.

Older Millennials—Who are we?

My dad is from the silent generation, my mom is a baby boomer, my brothers are Gen-Xers, and I am a millennial. However, when I joined the business world and sat through marketing meetings where millennials were defined as the target audience, none of the attributes of "millennials" resonated with me. Older millennials were born in the 80's and grew up mostly in the 90's. We had a lot of the "I don't give a crap mentality" of our older Gen-X siblings while life was easy and landlines were still installed in our homes. We came along just before part of our generation (the younger millennials) where everyone apparently got a trophy/participation medal and have spent most of our adult lives trying to argue the fact that we aren't millennials at all because we do not fit that prevailing descriptor. We remember the boredom of waiting to get through to our friends while being met with a busy tone every five-minutes. We remember feeling like our family was rich when we finally added "call waiting" to our phone plan.

We played with Tamagotchis, Skip-Its, Micro Machines, Bananas in Pajamas, Ouija Boards, Beanie Babies, Tickle Me Elmo, and like every good generation, Legos. We had Intellivision, Atari, Nintendo, Super Nintendo, Sega, Nintendo 64, Nintendo Wii, and PlayStation. We watched *Darkwing Duck, Chip and Dale Rescue Rangers, Saved by the Bell, Power Rangers, TRL, TGIF,* and *SNL.* A great day at school included access to the floppy disk computer where we got to play unlimited *Oregon Trail* and *Frogger* between typing lessons.

We remember the invention of the internet and transitioning from paper pen pals to email pen pals in late Elementary School. We can still sing the tune of dial-up as it cut through our phone lines and helped us log on to the world wide web. The greatest expression of affection for another was creating the best mixtape. In order to create one, we would lay on the bedroom floor during the *Top 20 Countdown* on Friday night and make sure that we hit record at the perfect moment to capture the song and then stop at the perfect moment so that we wouldn't get the radio talk show host's Voice on our crush / best friend compilation. We never knew what happiness was until the MP3 was invented and Napster allowed us to illegally create burned CDs instead.

We have AOL screen names and remember the flutter in our stomach when our crush would log on after a Friday night dance. We also remember the crushing agony when the *door close* sound occurred, and our that screen name turned italic mid-chat. Devastating. We know all the best 80's and 90's movies that we had to rent from the movie store on Friday night and understand the pang of horror when all copies had been rented. We wore Hang Ten, jelly shoes, wide leg jeans, belly chains, Sun-In, anything from the Delia's catalog, and Wet n' Wild makeup and our mother's would say "I used to wear that in the 60's/70's! I can't believe that's back in style!" Sound familiar? We remedied our caked-on foundation and frosted eye-shadow with Seabreeze and Clearasil as we entered the world of high-end skin care. We had frosted tips, acrylic French manicures, puffy dresses, tight updos, and tanning bed bronzed skin at our formal dances. We had thin eyebrows. Our sex education came from *Seventeen* magazine and *Cosmopolitan* as well as the original episodes of *90210* and *Melrose Place* during sleepovers.

We remember the evolution of cell phone technology starting with the brick phone our parents had installed in their cars to the first pay by-the-minute TracFones we used to call friends (when we weren't roaming). We remember every evolution of the iPhone and iPod since inception. We rode our bikes to school and to the pool in the summer with our friends unchaperoned and had sleepovers every night of the summer while sneaking out to play ghost in the graveyard with the neighborhood kids. We were the first 1M to join Facebook but didn't really like it at first because of the hard work we had invested into curating our top eight on MySpace. We grew up without a care in the world until we left college.

We grew up learning from our parents that the way to be successful in the world is to get a college degree, only to graduate with crippling student debt into the largest recession since the Great Depression. We were the first generation to begin most of our households with two working parents just as the cost of birth, maternal mortality rate, and cost of childcare in the United States rose to new heights. In high school, we lived through 9/11 and witnessed the way our country came together in the following days as "Patriots," then continued to watch our country get ripped apart over the next twenty years by religious leaders, media, and politicians that catered to fanatics and fear. We worked, homeschooled our children, and worried about our elderly parents through a global pandemic where some of our friends were laid off in the height of their career and many of us were prescribed our first antidepressant.

Every human experiences the disappointment of realizing that nobody is actually a grown up and nobody is really in charge when they become an adult. As older millennials however, we became adults just as every promise we had subscribed to about growing up became non-existent. It became incredibly expensive to get the same education our parents had without the job to take the next step to. Certainly, as women, we had access to more opportunities than our mothers, but the same rights our mothers fought for have still not been granted to us as we watch politicians attempt to stop the clock on progress for the sake of campaign dollars and votes. Starting and raising a family has become so cost-prohibitive that many of us feel like failures regardless of the choice we make.

The world has changed exponentially over the past twenty years due to the speed of innovation in both technology and communication. As the generation who has witnessed it unfold, we struggle to keep up and fit the bill as the majority generation of adults. Most people don't realize the oldest millennial is forty-two years old right now. We are the parents and the employees that are expected to carry the future forward, but many of us still feel like children trying to figure out the rapidly changing rules of a game we fear we will never win.

"Boy, does she sound like an entitled millennial or what? Get back to work slacker!"

I hear it, also not sorry AND I really did need to set the tone with the importance of a good, burned CD. Onward!

HOW DID WE GET HERE?

Identity Crisis: Social Media vs.
Waiting for Film to Develop

In the 90's, before cell phones and digital cameras, every school dance attendee came armed with multiple Kodak disposable cameras. Throughout the night we would snap pictures with our friends without a selfie in the bunch. Thirty posed snaps until the film would no longer advance. We could not see the image and adjust our pose. We couldn't go to our corners of the dance and scroll through images to edit and create the perfectly curated social media post about #bestnightever. It was just our friends, the moment, and our haphazard pictures which we forgot about immediately after they were taken. The next morning, we would drive over to the drugstore and drop off our disposable cameras to be processed and pay extra for twenty-four hours processing. We would sit in class the following week passing back and forth full stacks of printed photos, exchanging copies and reliving the fun of the night together.

Since the invention of the photograph in 1826, the medium has improved in quality, but the process stayed the same: point a lens at a subject, expose the lens to light, allow light to impart the image onto the film, wait for the film to develop. This process remained untouched for 149 years until the invention of the digital camera in 1975 by Steven Sasson, though this technology did not hit mainstream consumers until several decades later. The process changed again significantly thirty-two years later in 2007 when the first iPhone was released to the public (most older millennials were finishing or had already graduated college by then). Though digital cameras were still widely used in 2007, it only took a few years to shift again. Photos could be taken on a phone and immediately posted to social media, emailed, or texted to a recipient. This type of extreme technological advancement has affected most of the millennial's life experience, but I would venture to say none is more impactful to our identity and self-esteem than the advancement of photography and how we use it.

Now, there is no waiting and there is no reliving in person or sharing an experience intimately with our peers. We take a picture from our phone or two or twenty depending on angles, lighting, and double chins, and post to social media with the perfect description IF that photo is worthy enough to be on our main page. If not, it is posted for twenty-four hours to elicit reaction from our followers and then it disappears. The photograph's fate is staying unused on the camera roll on the cloud, where thousands of images live and are never used again. We refresh our phones throughout the day to see who has looked at our photo, how many likes we've received and if we have any comments or shares. Our perception of the experience itself is even slightly altered for better or worse, based on the reactions that roll in. Who are we, when even documenting and sharing our simplest moments in life are up for social feedback and validation? When we were at the mercy of developing film we were not able to edit and filter.

I owned a framed New Kids on the Block poster in elementary school that was, dare I say, my most prized possession. During sleepovers, my friends and I would take the poster off the wall when we were supposed to be asleep and take turns kissing our favorite members— Jordan, DUH! Our second favorite activity during sleepovers was attempting to get the attention of my Gen-X brother, Rich, who, if home, was in his room with the door closed. Maura and I went to see Hocus Pocus in the theater, opening weekend, and came back to my house for a sleepover. Completely inspired, we promptly dressed up in our best witch gear and gathered outside of Rich's room. Over the blast of "Smells Like Teen Spirit" behind his closed door we began to chant Sarah Jessica Parker's haunting theme:

"Come, little children, I'll take thee away
Into a land of enchantment.
Come, little children, the time's come to play
Here in my garden of magic."

He burst out of his room, and immediately, we knew the magic had worked! We screamed with joy as Rich protested, "MAAARG, what are you doing?! Get away from my room, or I'm going to flush your New Kids on the Block Poster down the toilet!!!"

This was not the first or last time he would make this threat. Of course, I now know that would never have happened because even if Rich had taken the poster out of the frame, he would have clogged the toilet so severely that my dad would have made him find a new home. Also, he was not that cruel on the inside, all marshmallow. Although I know these things now, in my 2nd-grade brain, all I could imagine was Richard flushing my beautifully framed masterpiece and reason for life down the toilet, and my existence in that moment would cease. I could not have gone onto the internet and printed out 1,000 new images of the band. I could not hop on my iPod and scroll through images on the band's Instagram account. There were no videos for me to watch on YouTube or documentaries for me to stream on Netflix. The only connection I had to my famous husband was his glorious music on a cassette tape, the doll released in his likeness, and his beautiful face framed on my pastel pink wall.

Now, we live in a culture of instant gratification. If I want to know who sang lead vocals to the glorious lyrics of "Step by Step," I can Google it and tell you, Jordan Knight, obviously. Also, it was released June 5, 1990 (THIRTY-THREE YEARS AGO?! THAT'S A WHOLE YOUNGER MILLENNIAL AGO!), produced by Maurice Starr, recorded at Unique Recording Studios in NYC, and sold more than 500,000 advance orders of their home music video, which made it the largest initial shipment of home videos for CBS Music Video. I worshiped NKOTB for years, and I just rattled off more information from a two-minute Google search than I have ever known in the band's twenty-four-year existence.

This is the identity crisis I feel when I hop onto the internet. I know that information is organized based on my previously searched preferences. I know I am fed images and content based on what I have looked at and read in the past. I understand that I am being fully manipulated by the incredibly addictive device I hold and the "authentic" influencers who show one side and forget to post the moment immediately following their video when they snapped at their kids or said something shitty to their partner. HOWEVER, a huge part of me wants to believe that everything is as sacred as the only two picture copies of my best friends and me on prom night.

I want to know that everything my kids feel from the social pictures they encounter is as genuine as the sweaty hair and shiny skin that only a disposable camera could perfectly capture. I want to trust that every exchange I have with an influencer on Instagram is as honest as the love I shared with Jordan Knight through that thin gold frame; and yet sadly, I know that it will never be the same. As an older millennial, I need to snap out of this tortuous identity crisis and come to grips with the inundation of social insanity we all face.

Goodbye, Jordan.

flush

Definitions

Google's English Dictionary provided by Oxford Languages

Authentic

Adjective

1. **Of undisputed origin; genuine: "the letter is now accepted as an authentic document" "authentic 14th-century furniture."**

Synonyms: genuine, original, real, actual, bona fide, true, veritable, sterling, attested, undisputed, rightful, legitimate, lawful, legal, valid, the real McCoy, the genuine article, the real thing, your actual, kosher, honest-to-goodness, pukka, dinkum, simon-pure

Antonyms: fake, spurious

In existentialist philosophy: relating to or denoting an emotionally appropriate, significant, purposive, and responsible mode of human life.

Why do we keep encouraging each other to show up as our authentic selves? Is that really what we want? I think it's important to be clear about what we mean by authenticity before we demand it of each other. I don't need to be exposed to everyone's fully authentic self in the way we currently define it. In fact, one of the major issues I see socially right now is the fact that many humans feel that it is their duty to show up completely unfiltered and unbridled with "Authenticity" as their mantra. I see authenticity in some cases empowering hate, racism, bigotry, and fear while it squanders empathy, understanding, love, and connection.

In some cases, we have lost authenticity as an inward, ongoing journey for truth, veracity, faithfulness, and accuracy, and we have put it on as armor for everyone else to have to deal with our most raw emotions and bad behavior. The biggest oxymoron in human behavior that I observe is authenticity as an act. We play our authentic selves on social media to challenge the "norm," only to struggle with our identity and harsh self-judgment on the other side. #blessed #livingmybestlife #authenticlife. We post pictures of ourselves in idyllic spots with the sun perfectly filtering our silhouettes after yelling at our significant other to "take another one" because we didn't like the way our double chin showed up a little too much in the first take. We assimilate authenticity with organic fabrics, makeup-free selfies, and crying on Instagram stories while assuring our followers that they #gotthis.

Actual authenticity takes a long journey back to who you were before the world got its hands on you. It takes a connection to spirit, surrender, self-love, self-acceptance, and self-parenting to get to a quiet and sacred place where we feel safe enough to get vulnerable to let out the smallest, genuine piece of ourselves and allow it to inform how we move through that moment then apply it to the way we move through the world. Our authenticity is not an "F you" attitude that we strap on before we log onto Facebook to protect ourselves from looking at the way we wear our pain and trauma. It is also not weaponizing our pain and trauma against others to teach them something we feel they must understand about the world through our experience. I've engaged in that behavior plenty of times. It has never resonated with who I am authentically, and it has never resulted in connection, understanding or progress.

At the beginning of the COVID 19 pandemic, I remember sitting in my friend's driveway. We were all on lockdown, and I hadn't seen her in months. As we sipped our Starbucks, I lamented about "[those people] who REFUSE to wear masks! What is their problem?! They say they can't breathe. C'mon, I can breathe; just wear the damn masks, ya know?!" "Margi," she stopped me, "Did you ever stop to think about what they are saying? 'I can't breathe' can be an indication of anxiety. Some people, say those who have suffered from abuse, have an incredibly difficult time having their face covered. Sure, you may be able to breathe, but that doesn't mean that other people are lying when they say they can't."

She was right. And I wasn't speaking as some authentic badass who doesn't take shit from anyone. I was speaking from authentic judgment, bias, and a narrow-minded perspective of my experience. Those are all authentic expressions of the shitty side of my awesome, loud, eccentric personality. Authenticity can be weaponized to make "us" right and "others" wrong. Have you ever wondered how countries can break out into wars where neighbors are willing to kill neighbors? Have you ever considered how close our own nation may be to that same dynamic? When people "other" one another for long enough, they begin to regard those who think differently less as humans and more as objects. It is much easier to destroy an object than a person. We are continuously on the verge of othering each other to death.

Some of our authentic selves do not need to be exposed to the entire world. Before we proclaim authenticity, we also need to be willing to take responsibility and examine, forgive, and grow the parts of us that have been broken, misled, manipulated, hurt, and overly praised.

To direct someone to "be authentic" will not elicit the desired result—assuming the person commanding even knows what they are encouraging. We need to stop directing each other to be authentic and admit that we live in a society where basically nothing is authentic. Maybe then, after a thorough exploration and admittance that we have no idea what we are talking about, can we all have a chance to show up as ourselves. That is not to say we don't have everything we need. Authenticity is simple by nature. It's in there for all of us as the truest expression of ourselves, but we have forgotten how to connect and access our authenticity.

Real authenticity is our undisputed, legitimate truth. It is not necessarily convenient or trend worthy. Getting to the truth can be painful and requires humility and vulnerability. One of the easiest ways to connect to our authenticity is to start to identify the parts of our lives where we have to pretend. Have you ever felt like you had to put on a face, a voice, or a certain way of being in a social situation? As I mentioned, most people struggle to show up as their 100% authentic selves. Sometimes those "fake" sides of us help us to adapt to certain social environments.

They help protect our ego from rejection or the pain and suffering that comes with the energy expelled in an authentic exchange. It's why we talk about the weather or laugh loudly at an executive's joke (even if it's not funny). It's why we smile and exchange niceties when we see acquaintances in the grocery store. Telling that person, "I don't want to talk to you right now because I'm in a foul mood today, and I didn't wear a bra because I didn't think I would see anyone I knew," might hurt their feelings or cause more pain for you than exchanging a thirty second volley about the unseasonable heat. You could also choose to have the described exchange and feel good because you behaved as your authentic self. Brutally honest does not necessarily equal authentic. A healthy society lives somewhere in the middle. Understanding who we are and what is important to us gives us a solid foundation for living authentically.

The rest of the details of our personality and life experience are also authentically ours, but they are not our core, and they can change. Think of the movie *"Inside Out"*. There are "Islands of Personality" held together by core memories (we'll touch on this in a couple chapters). As those core parts of ourselves evolve so can our personality. It doesn't mean we have become fake. It means we are growing. This is a healthy part of the human experience.

Our facades that we only put on some of the time are also authentically ours. People will judge you for who they think you are and who they think you are not. They will praise you for being authentic, and they will judge you for it too. The most freeing part about living authentically is deciding to be yourself in all your God-given glory while giving zero shits what judgment people cast on you. This doesn't give you permission to be an asshole. Well, I guess it does, but I implore you, for the sake of tolerable society, to show some discretion, know your audience and choose to serve others however you best know how. If you believe your authentic self and your sterling values are rooted in treating other people like crap or hurling defensive insults when someone disagrees with you, I assure you there are enough of you to go around, and the rest of us encourage you to dig a bit deeper.

Walking Contradiction

"Real isn't how you are made," said the Skin Horse. "It's a thing that happens to you. When a child loves you for a long, long time, not just to play with, but REALLY loves you, then you become Real."

"Does it hurt?" asked the Rabbit.

"Sometimes," said the Skin Horse, for he was always truthful. "When you are Real, you don't mind being hurt."

"Does it happen all at once, like being wound up," he asked, "or bit by bit?"

"It doesn't happen all at once," said the Skin Horse. "You become. It takes a long time. That's why it doesn't happen often to people who break easily or have sharp edges, or who have to be carefully kept. Generally, by the time you are Real, most of your hair has been loved off, and your eyes drop out, and you get loose in the joints and very shabby. But these things don't matter at all, because once you are Real you can't be ugly, except to people who don't understand."

—A conversation between the wise Skin Horse and the Velveteen Rabbit in "The Velveteen Rabbit" written by Margery Williams and illustrated by William Nicholson

I am now over three and a half decades old. For most of my life, I have subconsciously worked to figure out my niche. Who am I supposed to be? What is it I am here to do? As though I haven't been anyone or done anything up until now, and there is only one person I am some-how supposed to be and A thing I am here to accomplish. The ONE thing I am here to make happen. It used to be acting. I still have an undeniable sensation that at some point in this life, I will stand on the stage of the Kodak Theater and give the acceptance speech that I have written and rehearsed in front of many a mirror.

In addition to the one-purpose expectation narrative I either fabricated or absorbed over the years, I have also always felt the need to have specific defining traits which are not allowed to conflict with other parts of me. I am a Gemini, for crap sake. It's basically impossible to carry one theme for myself for more than thirty seconds, let alone a lifetime.

I was bullied most days in middle school. I was incredibly thin. I am 5'11" now with a 36" inseam and my legs were just as long when I was 12 years old and much shorter. I had no torso and in a bathing suit one could easily count my ribs with a casual glance. In my soul, I knew I was much more than just a skinny kid who looked like I was "starving to death"- their words, not mine. I knew that I was destined for the stage with an innate ability to sound out any song on the piano or make my family laugh by imitating all of the characters from my favorite films. I loved art and aspired to be Indiana Jones when I grew up. I loved church and going to my friends houses on Sunday afternoons. I loved Sunday night youth group and joining my friends on Tuesday afternoons at Hebrew school – especially when Daniel would get mad at me for raising my hand and answering the Rabbi's questions correctly. I begged to enroll in every summer camp my mom would allow me to attend, and I loved dance for 13 years until I started loving it less as I became aware of the ridicule aimed at me from classmates and their mothers regarding my appearance.

In my late teens and twenties, my motto was "I don't care what anyone else thinks or says about me." After ten solid years of being bullied by both kids and their parents for being "too skinny," the second my butt filled out on my five-foot-twelve frame and I had some measurement of boobs, I declared, "Fuck all y'all, I am a baby giraffe NO MORE!" and moved to NYC (well, I went there for college, but for drama sake let's pretend growing a butt made me go). The problem was that modus operandi never fully resonated with me in its entirety either.

I was raised to understand that while other people's senseless and meaningless judgment truly does not matter, integrity and reputation are important. In the early 2000's, guns blazing with two middle fingers high in the air, working three jobs, and earning my degree as I clubbed my way through the Meatpacking district the whole way to Williamsburg every night was fun (Ok, it was a BLAST with memories I will cherish forever) but it wasn't me showing up as my whole self. In fact, I abandoned parts of myself in the process of proving myself.

I was also in New York to pursue a career in acting. I had several casting directors interested in me, and every time I got close to an opportunity or had an audition for a job I was genuinely excited about, I sabotaged my chances by under-preparing, going out too late at night the night before, and waking up hungover or exhausted. There was a part of me who was clinging to mediocrity so that I could fit in, all the while suppressing the passion inside of me to be something huge.

As a thirty-seven-year-old woman with much to learn and owning the feeling that the second I have some sort of a clue what's going on, everything will change; I can say with certainty that there is one thing I know for sure: the beauty and intricacies of who we are lie in the dichotomy of conflicting traits. I am a walking contradiction.

- I don't care what people think of me, and yet, I deeply care about my reputation.

- I am a control freak who loves to delegate almost every task possible.

- I am easygoing and yet, not laid back but deeply passionate.

- I am an introverted extrovert (when I finally admitted this one, my head basically exploded, but it's true).

- I love to work, and I am constantly devising strategies that will ensure I will never have to work again.

- I love high-end luxuries, and I live in a crazy household with too much junk, four kids, two dogs, a bearded dragon and [I've lost count on the number of] fish, and I can certainly live without high-end luxuries.

- I am a Christian who meditates and believes the power of God and the Law of Attraction/theory of quantum physics co-exist (all contradictions...), who also has major issues with organized religion and feels most of the time that everyone is missing the point (...with an extra dash of contradiction).

The people who are *trying* to nail authenticity are missing the point. To be authentic, you do not need to pick a lane, be on-brand, or show one side of who you are. You also do not need to be unabashedly all parts of yourself at once. What's getting in our way is our strange obsession with being different and unique when we are in more ways EXACTLY LIKE THE PERSON NEXT TO US. None of us are different or unique, or authentic if we are desperately trying to fit in with and keep up with our peers. Remember that old Quicksilver ad from Surf Magazine? (I stole them all from my older brother Dan when he went to college and used them to fill my school notebook so I am quite familiar). It said,

"If you don't Surf, don't start." That's what this moment feels like to me. Trying to be authentic is killing our authenticity.

I grew up in a small town in Western Pennsylvania. It was an old steel mining town. Specifically, the same town where the epic rich kid/poor kid 80's classic "All the Right Moves" was filmed. Johnstown, Pennsylvania, was a booming steel industry town in the 1800's and was ravaged by a major flood in 1889. The entire downtown area was destroyed and rebuilt, only to get flooded again in 1977. By the time we moved to Johnstown in 1988, it was a quiet town with the downtown quite literally at the bottom of the hill, and the Hilltoppers, my school mascot, were the folks who lived in the old Victorian houses on the top of the hill. My school was known by surrounding schools as the snobby school. We had all the usual cliques so stereotypically defined that it felt like going to school in a John Hughes movie.

By the time I got to high school, I felt somewhat free and undefined. I always noticed that I wanted to be liked by the popular kids, but I undoubtedly had the most fun with the weirdest kids, the theater kids, and the music heads. In my freshman year, I found my way into the theater club and became fast friends with the seniors in our spring play. They collectively gifted me *Death to The Pixies*, The Pixies' greatest hits album for my birthday in June that year, and I sobbed at their graduation because I had no idea who I would be after they went away to college. They introduced me to the local rock 'n' roll scene, which put on awesome shows at fire halls around town. We would drive to shows in Brandon's 1989 sedan while Joie and Jacob (the only other freshman in the overly full car) smoked cigarettes and Jen and Roshni told elaborate stories in full character and sarcastic humor. We would dance uninhibited at the shows while bands rocked out and the doors of the firehalls were open and welcome to all. The first warm temperatures of the Appalachian June brought us the excitement of the summer ahead and we felt wild and unrestricted without any consideration for how others saw or did/did not approve of us.

The next year I was a sophomore, and I carried on the tradition of going to the shows. However, with my senior friends gone, the scene had changed quite a bit. The kids at the rock shows were trying to be incredibly punk and fit in with the vibe of Jimmy Eats World, The Anniversary, My Chemical Romance, and Death Cab for Cutie. They needed to prove to everyone that they knew more about music and that they were the most authentic in all the land. I remember the way younger participants would glare emotively with their arms folded, sitting in the corner.

They would stare and make fun of the popular kids who attended, "Oh my god, why are they even here? They are so fake. I feel so bad for them. They try so hard." My stock value went down with the new punk kids one Friday night when I overheard this boring rhetoric and responded, "Aren't you doing exactly the same thing? Trying to fit in?" I didn't attend many shows after that, but the experience set me up perfectly for the rest of high school.

As my best friend Sarah recalls, I unknowingly had a secret super-power and could look at everyone around me and see the game they were attempting to play and decide, immediately, I wasn't going to agree to those rules. This allowed me to be friends with everyone, and they could never punish me or shun me because I was never seeking their approval to begin with. Simply put, nobody knew how to handle me because I quite intentionally did not fully "fit in" anywhere. I had incredible friendships; in fact, my friends were, and still are, my family. I just didn't buy into the whole groupthink: "She doesn't like you, so

I don't like you; WE are all mad at her, so you should be too; she likes him, so you are not allowed to talk to him." No, thank you.

I wish I was more aware of this strategy at the time, but I think it was my mother who challenged me to attain this level of confidence. When I was bullied in middle school, my mom would always ask, "Do you believe them?"

"Well, it hurt mom; they chased me down the hall, making fun of my body, saying I looked sick and gross!"

"OK, but do you believe them? They will say all kinds of things. Technically they can say whatever they want to, what matters is if you believe them."

She gave me permission to "take the power back." By the time I got to high school, I had started to grow boobs (kind of), and in 10th grade, two of my [nerd/rock n roll/besties from 3rd grade] guy friends pulled me aside to inform me that they would now classify me as "hot." From then on, I gave zero fucks (for the most part…except for when I gave a lot of fucks…always a contradiction available). I still had plenty of relationship challenges, and strong moments of wanting people who showed no interest to like me as we all do, but I quickly refocused on my real friends and moved on. In hindsight, I had learned everything I needed to know about authenticity by that point. That same vibe is what carries me through life to this day, except as an adult I find myself giving the power back in situations where I feel insecure.

We all have pain and the same desire to be liked and accepted. It's what keeps society intact. What if we had permission to just be? What would it feel like to accept all of our messiness, our struggles, the "shoulds," "trys," "somedays," and "if onlys," and to forgive ourselves and adversely, celebrate who we are?

Let's lower the bar. You don't have to live out a three-sentence mission statement to be authentic. You also don't have to lob your entire heap of mess onto every table at which you sit (Unless you are with your friends and it's vent time. We all need vent time on occasion). Showing up authentically requires some introspection to first identify and understand your values. Most people I know would not list "inaccurately edited and uncited political memes" as a core value; however, many people I know brand themselves with other people's lies to fuel the advertising dollars of clients for Facebook, Twitter, and Instagram. Before you take on the next Amazon influencer's challenge to be your authentic self, take a moment to ponder your values.

What are the things you have come to hold sacred along your bumpy, painful, joy-filled, confusing journey through life? What would you consider your lighthouse through the storm of everyday chaos? How do you take your first step to resolve conflict or mistakes? We all handle challenging and rewarding moments where deciding is pivotal and communicates our authenticity to the rest of the world. Our values dictate what those decisions look like and how our pivotal moments play out. Some of us have solid values, and some of us have shitty values. On our road to connecting to our authenticity, it is imperative that we come to know and examine our values.

Start by writing them down. Once you take an honest look at your current values, it's ok to reflect in humility and decide to choose new values or get comfortable with the ones you already hold. Say one of your current values is "popularity," and as you sit with it, you admit that this is a value that does not serve you. In fact, it perpetuates judgment in your heart toward yourself and others, and judgment is something you would like to eliminate from your life! Write a new value next to the word "popularity" that will help to remind you where you are going, like perhaps "connection." It's ok to change course. It's ok to learn from your past and be honest with yourself about the BS you have been conditioned to believe to be important in life. It's ok to select new values.

As you reflect on your revised list, it may occur to you that within the past few minutes you completely contradicted one of your values by one of your actions. Uncovering your authentic self takes time, and you will screw it up by making mistakes or behaving in ways that contradict your values. Without a roadmap, however, you will be lost and remain prey to the expectations of what you *should* stand for that attack from the outside. Write down your values, read them, pray/meditate on them, and get some sleep. That was a big step. Becoming real isn't easy.

EXERCISE: Identify your values (and consider discarding the shitty ones).

1. Take out a notebook and write down your top five values. If you need to fill up a page with twenty or more values, then go through and circle your top five. Don't judge, just write.

2. Sit in reflection with your list. Underline the values that serve you and make you feel grounded. Try to resist the urge to label them "good or bad." For instance, I value Justice and Compassion. I also value Career and Abundance. Some may label the 2 latter values as shallow or materialistic. That's fine, they still belong on the truthful list of my authentic values which ground me and inspire me. Strike through the values that no longer serve you or create a sensation of guilt, shame, stress, or anxiety.

3. Challenge yourself to focus only on your underlined values and choose a new one to replace the ones that you are giving up.

4. Forgive yourself for not getting it right as you align yourself in the way you want to move forward. Mistakes are part of the authentic human experience. Owning up to your mistakes takes honesty, strength, and vulnerability. Authentic growth means you reserve the right to change you mind, seek new beginnings and move forward.

Some examples of values:

Abundance	Enjoyment	Happiness
Advancement	Encouragement	HardWork
Adventure	Enterprise	Humor
Affection	Endurance	Home
Balance	Excellence	Honesty
Beauty	Excitement	Innovation
Career	Faith	Integrity
Caring	Fame	Intelligence
Charisma	Family	Love
Change	Freedom	Involvement
Communication	Fitness	Joy
Compassion	Forgiveness	Justice
Connection	Fun	Kindness
Humanity	Generosity	Knowledge
Cooperation	Goodness	Leadership
Courage	Grace	
Creativity	Gratitude	
Diversity		

A Culture of Self-Righteousness.

"What might we be if only we tried.
What might we become if only we'd listen?"

—Amanda Gorman

The culture in the United States is completely polarized. Regardless of which "side" you are on, no one is saying anything of value. Or if they are saying something that we really wish the other side would hear, we know that the message will not get through because the other side has their mind made up, and they are too pigheaded or too stupid to understand what we have to say. I think most of us wish that things weren't so polarized and that we could collectively progress, but then we turn to the same media and social media that resonate with our opinion and continue to feel validated by the voices that echo our "personal brand," therefore proving the other side wrong once again.

It doesn't take long for us to realize that we know everything, and they know nothing. In fact, we know what is right not only for ourselves, but for everyone, and we call this "The Truth."

We demand authenticity from one another so we can judge each other and organize each other according to what we KNOW.

TO BE CLEAR: Our society has major, dangerous, systemic flaws, and I am NOT condoning them. Racism, bigotry, hate, and violence against the innocent are never ok, and there is no space for those attributes in what I am saying. I stand for Justice, Mercy, and Unconditional Love as Jesus **intentionally** taught and I believe we must be walking testaments to the future we want for our children.

I am instead making space for the idea that, for many of us, we need to do the work to heal and find a way forward in compassion with room for a beautiful range of thought with innumerable possibilities. Currently we are a polarized society. There is us and them; that's it.

This is where it might feel like I'm about to jump into politics, but please relax, that is not what is happening here. I will say, that I am confident as a constituent of the United States we have been unsuccessful as employers. Our politicians have failed us and our children in many ways and we continue to give them as much power as they will take begging for them to show us the way. Their childish behavior and inability to get things done has left them squabbling over ideas and buzz words that are not solutions to gain popularity and votes. If there is anything I want to invest the least amount of time talking about, its politics. That said, the current dynamic is toxic, immovable and we [the people] either figure this shit out or it will continue to be more of the same "us vs. them" bullshit where progress and critical thinking goes to die.

Now please shake that off. Walk around the room. Grab a glass of water. There is a lot of pain in politics right now and we are done talking about it. Instead, we are going to take several steps back and explore what it looks like to connect to our humanity authentically. We are going to dive in at an angle that requires openness on all levels, from all of us.

Currently, regardless of who we are, *we* understand the politics that everyone needs. We know the one true definition of who God is and what he or she wants for our lives. We understand the shortcomings of others and why they have "caused their own issues." We have all the solutions; if only *they* would listen to us because we are brilliant and all-knowing. Self-righteousness is necessary to being perceived as strong and smart in our culture. It is pervasive throughout our leadership and media figures. It is in our places of worship and is the backbone of our social circles. In our self-righteousness, we limit every corner of life and the defining relationships we are missing out on.

Let's reflect for a moment on the cinematic brilliance of Disney's *Encanto*. "We Don't Talk about Bruno" was part of the nightly dance routine in our home for several weeks after the film's release in 2021. One of the reasons it resonated so strongly with people in my generation is because we grew up on Disney movies where the villain was shamed, while we simultaneously identified with the villain. After watching *Ecanto* ad nauseam with our children and belting the soundtrack on repeat for the duration of every carpool, we were collectively reassured that most of the time, the villain is *defined* by the people who don't understand them. It's much easier to judge someone and label them as bad when we don't know the whole story or when we are in denial about our own reality. Since the beginning of our lives, we have struggled with a definition of bad or good. Intrinsically, many of us want to be good, which means most of what we feel is by opposition, bad.

We are human, but we hide our Badness by pointing out how others are clearly worse than us. Identifying the villain makes us the good guy. It also separates us from having real human connection and tortures us by creating a commitment to our shame. We must start by releasing our own badness so that we can see others as human. You are not bad; you are a living, breathing, beautiful soul having a human experience. They're not wrong; they are navigating the same temporary waters as you by either following or fighting against the sad excuse for a map that was laid out by the humans who came before them.

How many conversations have you sat down to lately that began with, "Let's talk about what we may not be understanding about their opinion?"

There is a dopamine rush that comes with the validation of being right. The entire model of social media depends on that part of our physiological response. If we could somehow identify that switch in ourselves and let go of the fear of being wrong, would we be able to listen, see each other, and define a future together that solves problems and supports each other as humans? Perhaps there is not one singular solution to every problem that has ever existed.

We are so used to proving each other wrong that we have not only forgotten what we stand for, but we question our own opinions if they differ from the resounding voice of our social network.

This subconscious need to conform is sneaky and embedded and feels just like that nagging question in the back of your head from middle school that sounded something like, "wait, am I allowed to like that person? Is it ok that I agree with them? What would my 'friends' say if I stuck up for this person in this moment?"

Here are some questions to shake things up. If these questions make you intensely uncomfortable, that's a good thing. I want you to like me, but that's not the point of this book, so you reserve the right to remain unchanged by this conversation and decide I'm just not for you. Sit in your discomfort if you can. If you find yourself judging the question itself, you may be experiencing self-righteousness. If you feel challenged and are willing to embrace it, try asking one of these questions in your current circle. Bonus points if you use your actual vocal box somewhere outside of social media.

Instead of Identifying and Shaming the Villain in the Following Situations:

- Is it possible for us to want different things in life?

- Is it possible that humans can authentically identify in "non-traditional roles" and feel called to raise their families by those guidelines?

- Is it possible that humans can authentically identify in "traditional roles" and feel safe in raising their families by those guidelines?

- Is it possible for women who resonate with traditional family roles to also support her sister, who is looking for the right (Constitutionally and socially) to achieve her own dreams and sense of equality outside of what we have previously defined as the "traditional way?"

- Is it possible that there are more effective ways to reduce _____ in the United States than by making _____ illegal? (These spaces are interchangeable if you find yourself in a fight for "anti" anything. I believe there is space for unseen solutions here too, in some cases).

- Is it possible that when a child is suffering at the mercy of a bully, there is more going on for that bully than that the parents have simply failed the child?

- Is it possible that God is bigger than the Greek text we understand him through as Christians?

- Is it possible we are comfortable being manipulated by the media, leaders, politicians, and social figures for the sake of their own self-interest, and we have forgotten how to think independently so we almost always look to others to define our truth?

- Is it possible that the heroes and institutions we grew up idolizing were also the sources of immense generational pain for many humans whom we choose to shut out because of our own guilt or shame?

- Is it possible that despite very real differences, we all basically want the same things? What are those common needs and wants?

How are you feeling? Open? Inspired? Triggered/Angry? Annoyed with a headache from the amount of eyerolling you just experienced? It's entirely possible that for you half of the answers to these questions are currently a resounding "NO." The challenge here is to open your heart enough to the possibility that the 1-3ish current solutions that we have scripted for some of the most pressing issues in our society are imperfect. So much of what we clash with in each other are our opinions, when authentically we often desire and need a similar result or outcome.

Can we hold space for more than one perspective at the same time? It is essential for us to first break apart our own narratives created by the voices that come at us in order to identify our unique understanding of the world around us. The world we love is filled with innovative solutions that came from a place of authenticity, necessity, pain, creativity, connection, and the humility to collectively admit in our humanity that things could be better.

In a time where society is forcing you to choose sides, choose to refuse to conform. Trust the ideas that come to you and form your own opinions. Authenticity is not about the image we curate, it is about the God-given perspective that is planted in our hearts and minds. Instead of needing to be right and constantly questioning the intelligence of others, what would happen if we questioned the messages around us and pursued the words on our heart by coming to the conversation humbly, knowing that the solution does not yet exist. Where might *we* be closed off or wrong? What outlooks exist that we may have never considered? We need your ideas. We need your innovation. We need your authentic point of view that comes from your soul which has had a completely unique existence. An existence which none of us can understand until you are brave enough to share it with us.

Grab your journal and write down some of your unique ideas. DREAM BIG! Stop yourself when you hear the voices you usually listed to on social media. Put those voices off to the side. These perspectives do not need to trend on any algorithm, but they do deserve the chance to breathe. They are yours. Not anyone else's. You have your own unique ideas and nuanced opinions buried beneath the believes you have learned to wear as armor. After writing them down read them to yourself and acknowledge your ability to create. That is what we are built for. We need to practice what it feels like to think and respond differently than the person next to us. We need do perform little acts of rebellion against the groupthink that we have become numb to. This starts with you. I don't need to tell you that you are "good enough" because you do not need my approval to bring your unique and beautiful perspective to the table without shame. Come to the table with your bravery intact, your ears open, your mouth slow, and your heart soft.

Just like Mirabel in *Encanto*, dare to be the one who, without approval and compliment from the outside, without a visible talent that awarded her with praise and popularity, was daring enough to seek out the difficult answers, listen where others were quick to judge, and think differently. Mirabel was the healing. She stopped the pain and created a solution amidst agony and destruction. This is not a time for more self-righteous "us and them" rhetoric, this is time to talk about Bruno.

"Alexa, play 'We Don't Talk About Bruno'"
[Intermission/ Dance Break]

Visceral Nostalgia

"You can't get there from here."

—*Deena Levy (Acting Coach NYC)*

I have an Instagram account where people are "encouraging" me every day to show up as my authentic self! I read books where authors remind me to wash myself, take life by the bootstraps, and simply be myself! I see magazines and catalogs of models and celebrities "without makeup" in effortless style, empowering me to live my best life. Shouldn't I feel like a daily beacon of authentic flow?! Apparently, I just need to listen to the chick with 115K followers and do my daily mantras and there I should be! So why is it so damn difficult and confusing?! Because it's all a load of BS. We are so obsessed with using the word "authentic" and being perceived as authentic that nobody remembers what authenticity means to them or, more specifically, feels like.

One of the ways we find and connect to our authenticity is through our senses. That is one of the reasons we are currently so confused. We are encouraged to numb our feelings and our emotions as we stare at our phones and ask ourselves, "Is this how I am supposed to feel?" Our senses act as wiring to help us remember, connect, and engage with who we are and why we are here.

It happens to me the same way every time. I push myself down the wrong path for any prolonged period of time. For example, at work I challenge myself and persevere down a disconnected trail of "should," "try," and "perfection," only to find out once again that none of those words actually mean anything, and I am left exhausted, overwhelmed and directionless. Then I end up needing to take an overnight in Duluth, Brainerd, or another Outstate Minnesota town that requires a long, flat, mindless drive. Along I go, letting my brain trail to my random playlist until "Landed" by Ben Folds Five turns on, and suddenly, I am transported to the summer after 10th grade.

Standing outside of the Metropol in Pittsburgh after a morning of taking my SATs, waiting for general admission seats to see Ben Folds. My brother had just brought my friends and me Ben and Jerry's Ice Cream because it's 95 degrees, and he was interning at a company near by, so he was in the area. I can smell my Gap perfume and see the length of my bootcut jeans paired with my FAVORITE army green halter tank.

After hours of waiting in the sun, we finally got in and ran to the front of the venue—we could touch his piano. Steph passed out at that concert from heat exhaustion, so we all started yelling for Ben Folds to stop playing because we could not maneuver back through the crowd to get Steph to safety. Ben stopped the show, confused by the yelling as we lifted her up onto the stage for the security guards to help. After she was taken to safety, Ben shrugged and began the opening riff to "Narcolepsy." It was the best concert of our lives, and Steph left with tour passes and tons of photos with Ben.

When I pop out of my memory, my arms are covered with goose-bumps, and tears stream down my face. Sound has this power over me. Music stores moments in time loaded with authenticity that I can pull off the shelf and access at any time, like a book in a library.

I call these experiences "visceral nostalgia." When we are lucky enough to experience a moment when all of our senses are engaged, and we are transported to another moment in time it is important to pay attention. When goosebumps pop up, tears well, your stomach falls out of your butt, and you can see, taste, and smell that moment in time, that is your authentic self-remembering, feeling, and connecting you through your vulnerability back to your truth.

When I was in acting class at Deena Levy Theater Studios in New York in the early 2000's, one of my favorite warmups required us to move freely as a group to an energetic song for a while and amplify the movement until we were fully exhausted, panting, and fully present in our bodies. We then sat in a horizontal line of chairs facing our teacher, Deena, with our eyes closed to do a chair-work exercise we called "sentence completion." Deena would prompt us with something like, "I love…," and then we would finish the sentence repeatedly until the prompt changed.

For example: "I love the snow, I love the sun on my face, I love my family, I love his hand on my back, I love to cry, I love to feel, I love the smell of bagels boiling first thing in the morning," then she would change the prompt.

After each of us moved through several of these prompts, she would turn on a song that resonated for all of us, like Joni Mitchell's "River," and tell us to close our eyes and go to our favorite place.

My favorite place every time was the dining room in the house I grew up in on Christmas Eve. Deena would give us direction to smell the smells and see the sights. I could see where everyone was sitting at Christmas Eve dinner with my Dad at the head of the table. I could smell the food, the candles, the fresh greenery, and even the seasonal bar of hand soap my mother put out in the powder room for the month of December. I could hear my bother Dan's infectious laugh and Richard's sarcastic quips. I could see the way my mom decorated the house to absolute perfection, like an editorial from an interior design magazine. I could see the snowflakes fall through the tall white French doors on our back deck in the glow of our motion detector lights because we lived on a cliff in the woods of Western PA, and deer were everywhere. I could feel my excitement and the actual warmth that grew in my body when I went back to that place. I could hear Amy Grant's Christmas tape playing on the intercom, and I could see the house perfectly lit with Christmas lights and soft lamps—my mom taught me everything I know about interior lighting. When Deena prompted us to open our eyes, every time, at least half the class had tears streaming down their faces.

In that 10-minute chair exercise we were transported mentally, emotionally, then physically to a place we felt safe and cherished. We were able to indulge in the corners of our memory that were authentic and unique to our experience. We were raw in a space where no filter or influence could alter our reality because the truth of these favorite places were stored in our bodies and emotions.

Our bodies are not meant to be shut off from our minds; our emotions are not meant to be shut off from our spirit; authenticity consists of our whole selves, including the parts that ache for a time in the past. The parts that are shut off or stored away. We can carry those parts with us too, and sometimes when times get hard, they feel like the safest and most cathartic versions of ourselves to tap into authentically. Let these moments of connection serve you. Let them bring you back to center to remind you of a part of yourself that may need to be nurtured, forgiven, or brought back in some way.

I am not suggesting we live in the past, but when we are lucky enough to experience heightened response to a memory through a form of expression like art, film, music, food, scent, or experience, we are plugging in to sacred part of ourselves. In those moments healing, clarity, manifestation, grounding, empowerment, and creation are all possible. This is the way we are designed. So, dig out those mixed CD's and turn up the volume. At the very least you'll have a good cry and some new ammunition to help prove to your teenager that you were once a cool kid too.

Self-Care and Other Four-Letter Words.

I cuss like a sailor, and I know I shouldn't, and I know it causes my kids to cuss like sailors, and my five-year-old just interrupted me as I was writing this sentence and said, "but Mom, dammit is not a bad word!" And that's all I have to say about that.

So now that we've covered my stance on most four-letter words, I want to talk about two words that really make my skin crawl: SELF-CARE. Self-care is something we preach as the solution to literally everything.

Has work been stressful? Don't forget to make time for self-care.

Having trouble in your relationship? Don't forget to take time for yourself. Self-care is really important.

Working from home during lockdown due to a global pandemic, stuck in front of a computer screen after back-to-back Zoom calls while your children are home from school, and now you are their teacher? Struggling from crippling anxiety that you have never dealt with before because you are perpetually worried about your loved ones due to the past three years of complete uncertainty and totally unclear as to whether or not life will ever be the same? Girl, make sure you take a salt bath and use a great face mask. It's amazing how much self-care can help!

I can't help but feel that society has watered down self-care to yet another expectation of women that has been reduced to a bath and a glass of wine. It's easy to feel like you are failing or falling short because you don't prioritize the world's expectation of self-care. It's time we redefine the meaning. If you have ever felt disconnected while taking time for yourself and even less restored after doing so, I get it. Over the past few years, after experiencing major failure, health struggles, a diagnosis of anxiety/depression, and most recently chronic EBV, I have learned something crucial about myself and my relationship with self-care: self-care for me means pushing myself toward faith.

It means identifying a challenge for myself that can only be accomplished by looking at the things that do not serve me directly in the face, offering them to God in prayer, and ultimately choosing what works and what doesn't. It means seeking growth. Currently for instance, that opportunity is my struggle with alcohol. Over the years, my "incredible tolerance" has dwindled down to *I have more than one drink at any sitting = inflammatory response that has me incapacitated for 1-5 days.*

I am presently in the negotiation stage with God on this one. How much alcohol can I drink and still be ok even though every doctor, nurse practitioner, and therapist has confirmed that my body can no longer process it? I *feeeel* like there has to be a way to "make it work", right God? (It's not going well for me). I also know sobriety is a phenomenal life choice for me because I have done it before for 6 months and I felt like superwoman. I know which way I need to go and self-care for me in this moment is abstaining from alcohol or admitting I can't do it by myself and getting the help I need. I'll get there.

 If we are open to growth, we are never past the point in our lives where new challenges and chances to learn are out of reach. Sometimes self-care means being honest, humble, and brave enough to take the first step toward growth.

To clarify, I have always loved all the relaxing and indulging actions that fall under the self-care umbrella. In elementary school, my friend Sara and I would spend every sleepover doing our nails and hair and trying new body sprays. By middle school, we were testing out my first face steamer, scrubbing our faces with shards of apricot seeds, and testing out homemade face masks from *Seventeen Magazine*. Sara now owns a bio-hacking company, where she uses what laymen would consider elevated self-care hacks to improve human longevity. She also has four degrees which make her qualified to do so. As I see it, from a non-professional position, when we very quickly prescribe each other self-care, we leave out an incredibly important detail around Mental Health and basic self-compassion. Why are we in pain? What is causing the stress and anxiety, or what is different about it this time?

In November of 2020, after several months of working from home with my four children also home, furloughing my team, living in quarantine, and perpetually digesting the same collective stress all humans were desperately trying to process, I went to my doctor for a routine checkup. It was my first time in Downtown Minneapolis in months since the riots following the murder of George Floyd. I parked several blocks away because I had not been to this office location before, and I felt unsure and unaware of my surroundings. I didn't know where I was going, and I ended up being ten minutes late, which made me more stressed than normal. I checked in, and I was asked for paperwork which I had not prepared. Once we got over that hurdle, I was led back to my doctor's office.

She walked in and said, "Hi Margi, it's good to see you! How are you doing?"

I live in the Midwest. "How are you doing?" is a nice question that people ask all the time as THE descriptive personality trait in Minnesota is "nice." This was different. She really wanted an answer. I could tell from her voice that she really cared. I looked at her and said, "fine," as I burst into tears and cried uncontrollably for a solid thirty seconds. She gently suggested, "You know what? I'm just going to have you fill out this extra questionnaire…"

 When the results came back, my Dr. asked, "Are you aware that you are off the charts for anxiety and depression?" "No," I responded. "I guess that makes sense after everything we've all been through. I felt as though I was holding it together as well as everyone else." She explained to me that sometimes PMDD (which I had been previously diagnosed with) can turn into sustained depression. This is also true for stress and anxiety. Sometimes things that are normally periodical can become chronic without awareness. She was right; I was crippled by stress, anxiety, and depression.

There had been days when I was unable to get out of bed, and I just chalked it up to a tough year where everybody was having a hard time. I had had enough self-care reminders shoved down my throat from social media and well-meaning friends and co-workers and I figured it must just be that I was not self-care-ing enough. I was prescribed medication and therapy, and within several months, I felt like myself again. As though a cloud had been lifted. I still have my full range of emotions. I can connect more truthfully to who I am inside without the unnecessary, unwelcome, and uncharacteristic fear. I can sit still in prayer with God and actually connect to the stillness and peace, whereas before, I was incapable of quieting my heart and mind for even a second.

There is a popular phrase in the female empowerment circuit on social media to help women feel like they are not alone during difficult times: "You got this!"

I get the sentiment, and while I understand that this is meant to be a positive statement, the truth is sometimes we DON'T got this. Telling someone who is struggling with depression, anxiety, or burnout that they "got this" without any specific recommendations, lifestyle/nutrition support, or, when needed, medication, can land like a lead balloon. It's a form of toxic positivity that insists, for example, that even if a new mother is feeling crushed by her new role and suffering from unrecognizable symptoms of postpartum depression, which is not only dangerous for her and her child but also completely treatable, she should just think positively, pull herself up by her bootstraps, and know that "she's got this!" For the record, that is not support; it's a form of silencing.

Our current definition of the term self-care is fine and can lead to a relaxing moment and can also be extremely dangerous if the expectation of what it should be doing for us prevents us from getting the help we need. Instead of guiding our friends and family toward self-care, maybe the first suggestion could sound something like this; "Hey, I'm sorry you're having a hard time. I know it's difficult to take time for yourself, but have you taken time for your mental health recently? There are lots of people and professional resources out there that can be helpful. Let's hop on Google together while we are waiting for our drinks to arrive and see what tools are right at our fingertips that we may not even know about!" General practitioners, counselors, therapists, Sanvello (App), Better Help (App) are all great places to start. If THOSE resources recommend self-care as the proper solution in a time of crisis, then you have an answer from a reliable source. We would not feel right telling our friend to just take ibuprofen if they clearly had a broken ankle with a bone protruding through their skin. We should not feel qualified to prescribe self-care for mental health issues.

When it comes to actual surface level self-care, I think that suggestion should also be followed with specific recommendations of lifestyle alterations that can help. I consider myself a professional guinea pig. Depending on my need for self-care, I have all kinds of tricks up my sleeve. I love to hop on Goop and see what Gwyneth recommends this week (don't you dare hate on GP, I'm an older millennial working mom and dreaming about summers accessorized with $750 Sweaters, $4000 boat shoes, vagina-scented candles, and $250 moisturizer with an IV bag in my arm IS my alley).

I then try said beauty hack and determine whether it's worth recommending to others. I love to read articles on internal medicine and alternative healing methods, and do all of them at the same time. An evening for me could look like this (in this order):

- Dry brush my body.

- Hop in my pop-up sauna for thirty-minutes while drinking copious amounts of water.

- Shower with a salt body scrub followed with glycolic acid face wash and a replenishing face mask.

- My favorite Jo Malone or Malin and Goetz candle burning.

- Scripture/bible study and a new journal.

- Dark chocolate and herbal tea.

If I'm really on my game, a workout at the gym or a walk around my favorite loop in the neighborhood will have preceded this ritual. If I'm struggling, in my two-week/month stretch of PMDD or in the midst of an EBV flare up, I may not do any of that. Out of survival, I will:

- Lock the door.

- Sit in the tub filled with bath salts.

- Stare at the ceiling.

- Lose an hour of my life scrolling on Instagram.

- Shove my face with chocolate or trail mix (with M&M's, duh. I'm not a monster).

- Micro-dose some THC with CBD.

- Watch a senseless Netflix episode or movie.

- Go to bed with or without brushing my teeth.

When we talk about "self-care," we need to think about Self-love and Self-Compassion. What do we need at the moment? Do we need a break? Do we need an appointment with a therapist or doctor to assess something that is telling us, in our gut, that something might be wrong? Do we need a new challenge to push through a season that has us stuck in our inauthentic self where we are misaligned with our purpose? We should encourage each other to start by trusting ourselves. If we are burnt out, what we may need are some hefty, healthy boundaries.

To be clear, I'm not advising anyone to ignore your bad feelings. I'm talking about going inward and connecting with who you are. I've learned that people think I struggle with self-compassion because of the way I communicate. I cringe when people say, "go easy on yourself," or "give yourself some credit!" I don't know what people mean when they say that to me. I am a critical thinker, and I tend to be very open about my perception of where I could improve or where I am struggling. I think this makes people uncomfortable, but I don't feel self-hatred when I speak critically about myself; it's my practice of reflection that helps me redirect my efforts or communicate my struggle and it's rooted in self-forgiveness and compassion.

If I'm genuinely communicating an area of struggle and someone replies with, "give yourself some credit, you have a lot on your plate!" my mind goes blank, and my face scrunches. Like, was... that supposed to be encouraging or helpful? I like to have a lot on my plate. That is my baseline. Telling someone to be *nicer* to themselves when they are vulnerably sharing their struggle can feel a lot like, "you got this!"

Self-Love is a respect that we need to hold for ourselves daily. In the bible, Jesus said, "Love your neighbor as yourself." It's one of those pieces of scripture that Christians like to hurl at each other to remind them of their humanity and to stop being jerks to each other. The issue is that some of us were never taught to love ourselves. When we became adults and felt the symptoms of a serious lack of self-love, we were prescribed the antidote of "self-care." However, this action untethered to self-love leaves us feeling like we just failed to feel something or properly accomplish the task.

Take out your journal. Write a love letter to yourself from the perspective of your higher power. God is an unending source of love, energy, possibility, and goodness. The Universe is the same untapped unending source of creation. Imagine God in the form of a voice. What does He sound like? How does it feel to hear His words of affirmation and love being poured out onto you?

EXERCISE: Feel Worthy of Self-Love and Explore Your Relationship with Self-Care

Take out a notebook and sit in prayer/meditation for any amount of time, opening your heart to the possibility of unending love. Write a love letter to yourself from your higher power (No judgment allowed. This is a total love fest).

Then trust your gut and take the next step. Book that appointment if that's what you need. Check in with your doctor or find a new one if you feel like you might be struggling with burnout, anxiety, depression, etc. Sometimes appointments can be a bitch to get, so don't hesitate to make a virtual appointment with any provider to get the ball rolling. Sometimes we *don't* got this, and we do NOT need to handle it alone.

Next, go back to your journal and get honest about your dreams and the life you want. What have you put on the backburner for your other responsibilities in life? What is one thing you can bring back into the spotlight to invest in yourself and in your joy? Is it a class, a degree, a book you want to write, a book you want to read, a social event you want to participate in, an instrument you want to play, a language you want to learn, or something else you have been putting off because it wasn't the right time or you had too much on your plate?

It's incredible how powerful it can be to write down a goal and take just the first step toward it. Conversely, perhaps you do not need a challenge—maybe the next act of self-care you can give yourself is taking something off your plate, setting a new boundary, delegating a task at work or at home, or even breaking up with a partner/friend who causes you pain. YOU have the power and ability to make decisions to serve yourself. If you need further encouragement, this is a great thing to talk through with a trusted friend.

Now, go sit in a bath, do a facemask, walk in the woods for thirty-minutes, work out to Metallica, laugh uncontrollably, ugly cry, or snuggle with something/someone you are grateful for. Any act of connection and care for yourself that is inspired by this message of self-love and God's compassion is yours to indulge in and celebrate. You don't even need to deserve it. It's free and you are already enough and worthy to accept it.

AUTHENTICALLY
FAILING

In 2016 I almost died giving birth to twins. Luckily, the three of us were in the right place at the right time, and I advocated for our survival, which led to an emergency c-section and subsequent recovery from an incredibly rare diagnosis of acute fatty liver of pregnancy. In the weeks following, I took on the undue mental, emotional, and financial stress of my unpaid maternity leave, and the clock began to tick on my twelve weeks of unpaid FMLA. My babies came home from the NICU after two weeks of care, and I spent the rest of my time at home with them, recovering from my emergency procedure and learning to care for my newborn twins.

One morning, while tallying up my bills, missed income, the difference in short-term disability pay if I had only made it to my annual review and raise, and the $3,000 I would owe my company upon return to work for employee contribution to my benefits, it occurred to me that if my husband had broken my ankle before I got out of the car at the hospital, I would have benefited from an additional week of short term disability as my fracture would have qualified as an emergency. My actual liver and kidney failure were not considered an emergency but part of pregnancy, labor, and delivery, so I had a "one-week waiting period" until my benefits kicked in.

I decided to start a company called Take 12. I realized that in all of my privilege as a white, educated, upper-level-management, good-money-making, insurance-card-holding suburbanite with access to amazing health care through a great company and transportation, that if I was feeling the pain and stress of unpaid leave, then every working mother was feeling it on some level. I was right.

Take 12 was an online registry where women could register for their unpaid leave, and friends and family could give them the gift of time in the form of cash contributions in lieu of a traditional gift registry. I collaborated and partnered with brands across the US (including Cora, Abby & Finn, Milk Stork, Gugu Guru, Every Mother Counts, Dove Men + Care, etc.) to help elevate the conversation around unpaid parental leave and created discount codes that registrants could utilize to purchase necessary items for the return to work, such as diapers, feminine products, and postpartum garments. I talked with hundreds of couples who were barely scraping by, balancing the desire and social expectation to procreate and grow their family with the desire and social expectation to contribute to the workforce, provide food and clothing for their children, and pay their medical bills.

The crisis was, and still is, undeniable. In fact, six years later, the US is STILL the only industrialized country in the world without federally supported paid family leave besides Papua New Guinea. I created a tool that truly addressed a need and was working to develop it into an insurance product that companies could utilize to organize and support paid leave within their organizations. Then, my health failed. 2019 was the worst health year of my life. I ended up in the emergency room over six times with different ailments that required multiple tests, treatments, and follow ups.

I was working myself sick, and my body was screaming at me to stop. I knew I was pushing myself hard on an uphill battle, but if I could just get the product to a place where we could get our first major corporation on board, I knew the investor money would follow, and my B2B model would be off to the races. The fall of 2019 was my make-it-or-break-it stretch. I presented my plan to launch my new business model with the last few dollars in the banks at my late November advisor board meeting, and I was ready to make it happen.

Two weeks later, I had a supplier meeting in Duluth for work, and I woke up with a stomachache. I figured it was something I ate the night before, popped a TUMS, and hit the road. By the time I was headed South on my two-and-a-half-hour drive back to Minneapolis, the pain was so excruciating that I had to pull over in a McDonald's parking lot and take a forty-five-minute nap with my car running to keep me alive in the balmy -10-degree tundra. The next day I laid in the hospital on Dilaudid, recovering from my appendectomy, and waved my proverbial white flag. I was finally listening. It was time for me to admit that my health was more important, and my work with Take 12 was done. In that moment, I decided to quit what I had poured my heart, soul and healing into for the past four years, and I took on the statistically popular title of "Failed Startup."

I was heartbroken and humiliated. Embarrassed and scared of what all of the people who had believed in me, supported me, and invested money in me along the way would say. Perhaps I was even more scared of the folks who had already rejected the idea and pre-judged that it would never work or amount to much. I had failed. I didn't finish what I set out to accomplish. I believed so deeply in Take 12 and its ability to help people and change the world. Failure was never an option until it happened. I had failed.

Two weeks after my surgery, I made the first phone call to one of my investors. She was a woman I had come to admire deeply and had come to call a friend. I was devastated to call her and admit that it was time for me to begin the shutting-down process. I told her honestly, without excuses and without shortcuts and her response took the wind out of me completely.

"I completely understand. I'm sad that it has come to this, but I'm proud of you, and you should be proud of yourself too." The three investor calls that followed went similarly. None of them were angry. Nobody said I told you so, and nobody hung up the phone on me. They knew I had given it every last bit of myself and that I remained committed and fully invested until the last second. They could feel my authentic passion and had invested in me, and I had not let them down.

Why are we terrified of quitting and failure? Older millennials have worked their entire careers against the narrative that we are lazy, entitled complainers who want everything handed to us and who demand a trophy with everyone else. I struggled my way through school sports from 1993-2003, and I never once received a trophy. When I joined the workforce and learned that the millennials were known as the "everyone gets a trophy" generation, I became resentful. Is there someone I can talk to about the trophies? Am I still eligible? I see a generation of humans who have worked their asses off from the second they graduated into the largest economic crisis since the Great Depression. I see the fear of risk-taking and clench on security that has never proven itself. The second we do not achieve perfection we deem our work failure and dismiss the incredible work that preceded that moment of quitting.

I had helped hundreds of women and couples who had no voice against the cultural norm that demanded them to have babies, keep their jobs, and figure the rest out. I comforted a woman who experienced extreme loss and who used three days of bereavement pay to recover from her nine-month pregnancy because her maternity leave was no longer available to her when their child arrived stillborn. Take 12 provided agency for parents who spent their leave in NICUs, hospital rooms, or at home, struggling through postpartum complications, depression, and even joy, that they did not want to rush away from to get back to work as quickly as possible. My work was important, it helped people, and it inspired others to give a shit. Where was the failure? Take 12 did not make it to insurance brokerage platforms. We did not raise a Series A round of investment. We were not acquired for $20 million. But the thousands of conversations, meetings, presentations, pitches, incubators, customers, partnerships, and customers who engaged were the successes of Take 12.

After processing this I have come to accept the great accomplishment that creating and running Take 12 was. I have added it to my resume. I have become a coach and adviser to other female founders who have the courage to dare and take on complicated problems and improve peoples lives through innovation and business. Take 12 taught me more than I could have guessed. It made earning my MBA a cakewalk (exaggeration) and it proved to me that I can not only do hard things, but I can teach myself how to do new things! Millennials have lived long enough to fail. We are badasses and are now in our 30's and 40's. We are not children who need to feel subjugated by the adults in the room. In fact, there are no "adults" in the room. This is it. Let's encourage each other to pick up our failures and carry them with us. Decide what you have learned and how it can propel you to the next step. I would never exchange my experience with Take 12 for anything else. I value my failure and I wear it proudly.

HUSTLE PORN

How many "authentic" influencers does it take telling me to wake up early for me to actually become a morning person? Like the Tootsie Roll, Tootsie Pop, "The world may never know." Actually, I do know. ZERO, because it is never going to happen. I believe you can be successful in life and still prefer to sleep in, value downtime, keep your current job, love, and be loved by your family.

Hustle Porn is my term for the culture we see in social media especially aimed at entrepreneurs or those searching for a way to make a living outside of the traditional 9-5. In the jaded section of my mind, Hustle Porn is represented by the voice of young "bros" who have accomplished something in a time of their lives when they were broke, single, and accountable for very little outside of themselves. (I warned you about generalizations. I suppose this is also a stereotype, but you're stuck in my brain for the moment and this image is representative of my experience. No apologies.) It is projected onto women but does not account for the added work a woman takes on in society as a caregiver, homemaker, and more recently, breadwinner. It's addicting to watch because these voices tell us that if we are willing to sacrifice everything, we can accomplish anything!

Admittedly, I have a strange relationship to this narrative. I love to produce and accomplish. After much therapy, soul searching and reading about my enneagram type (3W8, duh), I have accepted that I love to have a lot on my plate, and I do better when I don't have to be hyper-focused on one thing. I love to achieve things, and a solid challenge is in every way self-care to me. However, the notion that we need to try as hard as we can and never give up and never give in to failure has always felt like bullshit to me, as well as horrible rhetoric with which to attempt to empower women.

I am a starter with an idea a minute, and I love to fill my brain with hacks and tips about productivity, focus, and "making it happen." Most of what's out there is nonsense, but when I land on a podcast or interview with someone I admire, I listen, as most of the advice revolves around creating healthy boundaries, healthy habits, and creating minimum viable products instead of killing yourself to build an empire from day one. Thinking about what you want, testing it, and scaling with healthy boundaries in place for steady, sustainable growth is an option. Honest reflection that leads to trashing components of your plan in order to unvail a new way forward is a gift that is also available to you. It can be an excruciating process in spaces where ego leads the way as humility is required. Getting to what works is a process of peeling back the layers of shoulds, supposed to, and trying in order to uncover the truth.

"Margi, are we talking about start-ups or life here?"

Yes.

When I built Take 12 I learned that anything can be built fifteen minutes at a time. I built the company while working a full-time job and raising four small children. I could not afford to be dead in order to make my company a success. To be fair, I ended up having to shut down Take 12 after four years, but I don't believe for a second that my failure had anything to do with my commitment or effort. While building and running Take 12, my daily to-do lists were like chapter books. In order to not feel overwhelmed, I would bracket my tasks in fifteen-minute increments with larger brackets for things that required (and warranted) more time and full attention. I was able to make crucial phone calls, send emails, write copy, send edits to the developer, respond to customer needs, and create social media content in fifteen-minute bursts. If I had waited for uninterrupted brackets of time, I would never have been able to start. (I called upon this way of working once again during COVID work-from-home/ homeschool/ lockdown madness. It kept me functioning... and employed).

While fundraising for Take 12, I met with young men who worked for investment firms, and they would say that they could never invest in me until I was "fully committed." This feedback would enrage me, as, from my perspective, I was more committed than anyone I knew, but from their single bachelor, Hustle Porn addicted point of view, I was only partly committed until my children had no grocery money and my marriage was holding on by a string. I didn't buy it then, and in hindsight, I don't buy it now. In fact, I couldn't help but have the same adverse reaction any time I was met with this response—if I had been able to accomplish THIS much in the little spare time I had to work with and everything on my plate, what did these dudes do all day?!

We don't have to kill ourselves to create something great or even live the simple, beautiful life we have always envisioned for ourselves.

Exhaustion and burnout do not make great employees, entrepreneurs, partners, parents, or members of society. My new #Makeithappen slogan is around creating healthy boundaries, prioritizing health, and finding gratitude and contentment in the work you are doing NOW while following your loudest dreams and allowing them to change as you change.

Sometimes I wonder if we love to hate today's current hustle culture because it shows us an image of who we never want to be, which allows us to excuse ourselves from being 100% successful. We don't need to subscribe to social media's definition of success, but there is something so pleasurable in torturing ourselves with the self-made billionaire stories that insist we need to kill ourselves trying to ever get a taste of what they have. That delicious clickbait that tells us we need to work harder and sleep less than everyone else to be successful is like watching a train wreck disguised as someone who claims to want to encourage us, and the truth is, we have no idea what their life is like when the cameras are off. We can judge, positively or negatively, but with even the most "authentic" hustlers, we don't really know what their life looks like.

The bottom line is that we all need to define our own success and stop looking to strangers to tell us what we are missing.

LADIES—This is my attempt to reframe #hustleporn #makeithappen.

To be clear, WOMEN, you can do ANYTHING! I know you have had someone in your life tell you something you wanted would be too hard, or take too long, or be too challenging with all of the other things on your plate. I know that you have had many conversations about all of the responsibilities in your life only to be met with, "wow, you're BUSY," with so much judgment it felt like an accusation. I understand that you are not looking for an easy way out, and in order to build something, you also feel the legitimate weight of responsibility to make it work for your children and/or partner in order to feel justified in the path you have chosen or challenge you have accepted.

Let me say it again: YOU CAN DO ANYTHING!

The world will never stop telling you how you should feel or what it should all look like, but you can take on as little or as much as you want as long as it is serving you and your ultimate growth in mental, emotional, spiritual, and physical (I'm still working on this one) health. **It doesn't have to look the same way it did for the man who did it before you.** You can settle down, then un-settle down, then settle down again—all of those terms are bullshit! You are a growing creature, and you will require different paces at different times of your life. If at any point you feel like your world is falling apart from a dream you once craved more than anything, it's ok to admit failure and reiterate. Failure is not a dirty word; rest is not the opposite of achievement; hustle is not equal to success. **Do anything. You can do anything.**

THIS IS ADULTING

Finishing this book has looked like me starting, stopping, scrapping, starting again, rewriting, stopping, completely changing, starting, stopping, starting, procrastinating, self-sabotaging, asking my best friends to hold me accountable, stopping, rewriting, stopping, starting, and finishing, since 2016. The complete version of this book was originally over 35,000 words and after several conversations with publishers who asked me how I wanted this book to further my career, I decided to take it in yet ANOTHER direction. Creating a niche-based startup around this book felt limiting and inauthentic.

In writing this book I can finally articulate that I am not best served, nor do I serve best, in a niche or a "lane". My voice is relevant and evolving and the unique lessons I have to teach my peers are varied. The solution? This book. The rest of my content will live on www.NoNiche-Woman.com. I will continue to do my best to evolve and contribute to others by refusing to cap the conversation here. This mini-memoir is just the beginning.

Every word in this book comes from a genuine and vulnerable place inside me, and I have been astonished by just how difficult getting some of my own authenticity onto paper could be.

I'm writing this last section on a Tuesday night five days before my 37th birthday. My husband is snoring triumphantly in our bed behind me, and our older kids are stomping around downstairs, probably making "second dinner." (9 months after writing that sentence, I am now doing *final final* edits on a Tuesday night, husband still snoring, kids still second dinner-ing. This is most certainly adulting.)

I am grateful for the time you have spent with me to read these words and consider your own perspective. My hope is that you share this book with a friend whom you may have had a similar conversation with, or even better, a friend who needs to shake it up. I know that our ability to listen to each other and start new conversations is the way that this generation has already started to change the world. It is crucial that we continue to define how amazing the future can be for our parents, for us, and for our children and grandchildren.

We don't need to try to contextualize what's not working into an old broken framework. We need to be brave enough to put our egos aside, consider each other's pain and connect with those who are different than us in order to move forward and create real change. We don't need to accept "well, that's just the way it is" in any arena of our lives, and we simultaneously don't need to fight every single opposing opinion if we disagree. All fights are not weighted equally, and some require our gifts, passion, and commitment, while others are not our fights to fight.

Remember that we are all humans, and at the end of the day, we have the same raw basic needs. Remember that you have resources and agency, and you may need to advocate for yourself, your health, your children, and others around you who cannot advocate for themselves.

Remember that the divide between "us and them" is exactly what *they* want. To be radical, we must bridge the divide and challenge the polarization. Challenge and define what you stand for. Adulting is hard and even harder for those who face injustice, prejudice, hate, and ruthlessness every day. Stand for REAL Righteousness, Justice, Compassion, and Mercy.

YOU are the adult in the room now, and YOU have the power to stand for what is right and good while teaching the children in your life how to do the same. We need you to show up as your authentic self, and YOU are the one who gets to uncover who that is.

I encourage you to value your thoughts and pay attention to what makes you angry and where your passion pushes you. I encourage you to use your words and to show up in vulnerability and talk about the difficult things that set people off in a new way, rooted in compassion for their pain and experience in life. I implore you to do the hard work on yourself when you are ready, and in the meantime, give yourself grace and comfort for all you have been through. It's ok to sit with your pain, even when it is excruciating. You are strong enough to dig deep and uncover the parts of your pain that are holding you back and find compassion for yourself for the pain you are not ready to let go of. It's ok to ask for help to get to the other side.

This is an incredible and beautiful life, and it's time for us to show up as adults with parts of our child-selves leading the charge. We have unique journeys that no adults before or after us share. We need to bring the part of us that knows freedom, endless summers, living on our bikes with no tracking devices, watching the world grow/expand/

and connect through technology while we grew alongside it, and help take society to the place it deserves.

Thank you for taking the time to read my book! I hope you gained some new insight and feel inspired to take the next step in showing up as your full, authentic, unapologetic self. For inquiries on speaking events or private coaching/mentoring, please reach out on NoNiche-Woman.com.

I look forward to connecting with you and continuing these conversations.